# PROTOTYPE FOR A PLYWOOD WHEELCHAIR

© Copyright 1999 Marco Steinberg

All rights reserved. No part of this publication may be reproduced without permission. The work herein is that of individual authors; it does not represent the views of the Graduate School of Design, Harvard University, or any of its programs or faculty.

International Standard Book Number
0-935617-46-9

Library of Congress Catalog Card Number
99-073726

Published by Harvard University Graduate School of Design

Printed in the United States of America

Copies of *Prototype for a Plywood Wheelchair* are available for purchase from:

Harvard University
Graduate School of Design
Book Orders
48 Quincy Street
Cambridge, MA 02138
617.496.5113

Cover image drawn by Mark Careaga

# PROTOTYPE FOR A PLYWOOD WHEELCHAIR

MARCO STEINBERG

with a preface by Peter G. Rowe

# TABLE OF CONTENTS

|  |  |
|---|---|
| Dean's Preface | 7 |
| Introduction | 9 |
| Design Premise | 10 |
| The Wheelchair | 13 |

**15 PLYWOOD'S LINEAGE**

|  |  |
|---|---|
| What is Plywood? | 15 |
| A History of Plywood | 17 |

**25 BENTWOOD PRECEDENTS**

|  |  |
|---|---|
| Samuel Gragg: Side Chair | 26 |
| Isaac Cole: Patent Model for Plywood Chair | 28 |
| Michael Thonet: Experimental Chair | 30 |
| Alvar Aalto: Paimio Chair, Earlier Version | 32 |
| Gerald Summers: Armchair | 34 |
| Charles and Ray Eames: Wood Splint | 36 |

**39 PLYWOOD WHEELCHAIR PROTOTYPE**

|  |  |
|---|---|
| Applied Research | 43 |
| Process | 45 |
| Fabrication | 47 |
| The Mold | 49 |
| The Laminate | 49 |

**53 COMPONENTS**

|  |  |
|---|---|
| Base | 55 |
| Armrest and Control Panel | 59 |
| Seat and Footrest | 63 |
| Backrest | 67 |

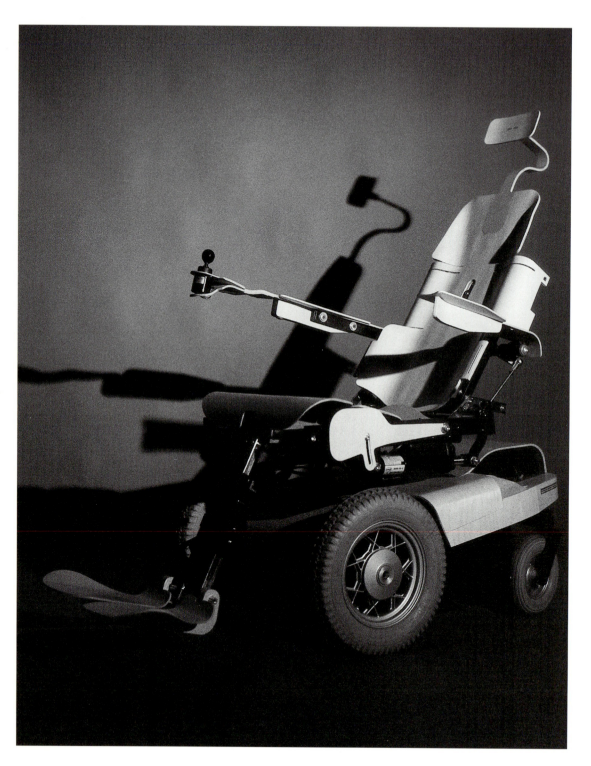

## DEAN'S PREFACE

For some time now, the Harvard Design School has become more actively involved with matters of industrial design, special materials, and alternative methods of fabrication. This new focus is partly reflected in the recently endowed Snyder Prize for Innovation in Design and Fabrication; the work of the School's Center for Design Informatics, especially in areas such as computer-aided design and computer-aided manufacturing; and the creation, in 1997, of the Design Arts Initiative aimed at bridging the gap between areas such as industrial design, interior design, and traditional architectural education. Clearly, the advantages to be gained from these efforts are substantial, particularly in view of emerging opportunities in professional practice, accelerated developments in building and building-related technology, and a very keen interest on the part of students and faculty to explore the new frontiers of this rapidly evolving set of interests.

Marco Steinberg's Plywood Wheelchair Project was both a response to this new involvement within the School and a significant point of reference for subsequent exploration and initiative. Executed at a time when stronger and better focused attention on new materials and technologies was in the offing, Steinberg's project is a splendid example of this potential—proving not only conceptually helpful but also raising the level of confidence that can be shared about a new initiative. This reciprocal developmental aspect of the wheelchair project warrants pointing out because it so clearly shows how advancements in academic fields of interest occur not only from general speculation and analysis of apparent shortcomings, or 'gaps,' but also from very specific research projects with no real prior intention to alter a broader institutional perspective.

Steinberg and his colleagues' work on the Plywood Wheelchair Project is a clear demonstration of how design innovation can make timely and potentially lasting contributions to pressing real world problems. In this case the world of those physically challenged is enhanced and, in Steinberg's own words, technology becomes a 'catalyst for human possibilities rather than a restricting factor.' The project also shows how a relatively traditional and common material—plywood—can be reconsidered as a high-tech substance, especially when embedded with smart control devices and when it becomes the product of an advanced design and manufacturing process. It also demonstrates how the pursuit of beauty and practicality are neither lost arts nor mutually exclusive. One of the prospects of new materials and fabrication methods is that a designer can do almost anything with them and, therefore, the aesthetic dimension of the matter of taste becomes all important. However, when used at or near the limit, conditions either of material preface or fabrication, function, and appearance must once again become inextricably bound together through design.

Finally, research projects like this one require considerable support not only from their host institutions but also from other interested parties. The Design School wishes to thank Permobil USA, Inc., which served as the client, and Lionheart Gallery in Boston, which participated in concept initiation and was actively involved in the grant development. Larry and Laura Snyder, through their annual award at the Design School, were also instrumental in advancing the project.

Peter G. Rowe
*Dean, Faculty of Design, Harvard University Graduate School of Design*

INTRODUCTION

This project—to design and fabricate a full-scale prototype of a motorized wheelchair made of wood—was commissioned by the Swedish company, Permobil, a pioneer in wheelchair development. Familiar with the Scandinavian tradition of using wood in mass-produced products, Permobil was interested in exploring the material's potential for its own production.

Thus challenged, we followed our design instincts, directing the research toward the creation of a new paradigm. We focused on plywood because—as both a natural and an engineered wood product—it held the promise of reconciling the technology of the wheelchair with the humanity of the user. Given the existing chassis and electrical framework of Permobil's standard wheelchair, we developed a new kind of plywood skin by housing the technological and structural elements in the wood's laminations. The result was a multidimensional surface combining the tactility of wood with the technical and mechanical needs of the user.

This interdependence of form, materials, and function helped us to conceive the wheelchair not as a technologically determined product, but rather as a catalyst for human possibilities. The research also suggested that a new, technologically advanced plywood could match plastics, ceramics, and metals in terms of its potential for a wide variety of applications and products.

Working from June to September 1997, we conducted our research in the spirit of informed imagination, testing hypotheses and learning from our mistakes to see new possibilities. The computer served us as both a design and a fabrication tool. Ultimately, we developed a computer-aided fabrication process that allowed complex plywood forms to be fabricated in an automated environment and manufactured two identical prototypes of the chair.

DESIGN PREMISE

As an act of "form giving," designing can be an elusive process, but it is far from gratuitous. Through designing, the complexities of the context and program are given shape and fleshed out in the physical world. It is during this process that we need to inform, and be informed by, those complexities. We need to inform form so that it can aquire meaning.

Gaining presence through matter, form has real physical and quantitative characteristics. Without this quantitative aspect, the qualitative can only have symbolic meaning. It is therefore critically important for designers to understand materials and fabrication processes in order to infuse form with meaning.

Since the advent of industrialization, fabrication and design have usually been two distinct processes that rarely inform one another. These specializations have produced a proliferation of materials, technologies, and objects whose meanings and values have not been fully understood or explored. As a result, materials have often been assigned reductive—that is, predominantly aesthetic and/or structural—values.

The issue is far more complex than a simple qualitative versus quantitative dichotomy. Insofar as it exists in the built environment, form inextricably binds design and fabrication. The inability to bring to resolution the full complexities of material, fabrication, and design has resulted in a proliferation of apparently sophisticated, but in fact unsophisticated, products.

> The sheer range of materials and techniques with which it (modern industrial civilization) confronts the designer is staggering...They (materials) are available everywhere, to everyone; not a craftsman or designer in the western world can be unaffected by their presence. And yet their presence is by no means fully understood. Their physical properties are very complex, their aesthetic properties even more subtle and less explored. They are dumped upon the designer in such an accelerated flood that he has little opportunity to explore and master them in either practical or aesthetic terms.[1]

The advent of computer-aided design and manufacturing (CAD/CAM) systems has brought about a radical transformation in the design world. It has created a direct means by which design can again become an integral part of the fabrication process, intertwining the "qualitative" with the "quantitative" and revolutionizing the designer's relationship to materials and manufacturers. It is precisely this new potential that we explored in the wheelchair design, developing in the process a new spectrum of possibilities for using plywood.

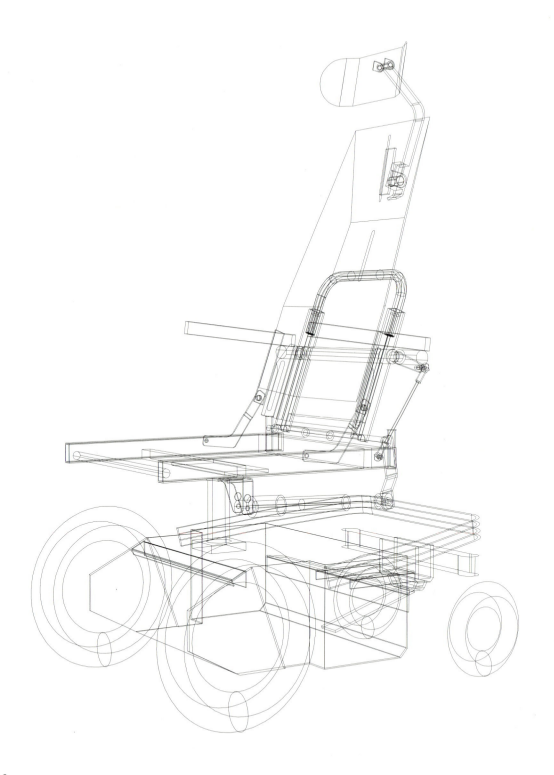

## THE WHEELCHAIR

With its complex technical and social demands requiring a perfect resolution of both the quantitative and qualitative, the wheelchair provided an exemplary case study. Its design has, for the most part, focused on engineering as a means to accommodate the body; as an engineered artifact, the typical wheelchair is primarily a mechanical device. The wheelchair, however, needs to address not only the mechanics of the body, but also the culture of the user. Frequently seen as a way to humanize the chair, form has been draped over it as a cover to aestheticize the mechanical, which often results in a highly disharmonic relationship between user and device. The distinct attachments, features, boxes, wiring, tubes, and bolts necessary for its operation make for a highly discontinuous design. The primary presence of the wheelchair is not experienced through a seamless interface with the user, but rather through the seams, or devices. As an engineered product, generated and defined by quantity, the wheelchair has always embodied the idea of limits.

By virtue of the resolution of both quantitative and qualitative issues, furniture is the embodiment of new possibilities. Reconceiving the wheelchair we transformed it from device to furniture. In doing so, we looked at both the current state of technology and at history.

The historical component of our research, however, did not consist of forms to be copied, but rather principles to be understood, spanning the spectrum from prosthetics to furniture. These principles informed the design of a simple chair form, with simplicity understood not as a reduction, but as a resolution of complexities.

# PLYWOOD'S LINEAGE

Plywood derives its lineage from numerous traditions and manufacturing processes. As a material, it maintains allegiances to wood and woodworking traditions. As a product, it has roots in laminar and industrial processes. The richness of its history, from antiquity to today's latest advances, endows this simple product with presence.

## WHAT IS PLYWOOD?

*Plywood* refers to an assembly of thin slices of wood sandwiched together in a way that transforms characteristics of the raw material into strengths and assets of the product. These slices, or veneers, are glued together in layers of alternating orientation and pressed to form the plywood sheet.

Plywood as a material, however, begins its process in the trunk of a tree. It is here that we find wood in its natural state, organized as a bundle of vertically running fibers. These fibers, much like straws, bring water and nutrients from the ground to the leaves. The walls of the fibers are made up of living cells, which like all living organisms are water dependent. When wood reaches its "water saturation point" (referring to the maximum water retention capacity of the wood cells) water will fill the fiber cavities. Likewise, drying will result in a water loss from the cells promoting a dimensional change in the wood. A change in air moisture content in dried wood will either increase or decrease the water in the cells, causing the wood to swell or shrink. Such shrinking and swelling of wood may not only change the wood's dimensional characteristics, but can also cause it to bend or split. Furthermore, swelling and shrinking occur predominantly with respect to the diameter of the fibers, not their length. Therefore a sheet of wood will tend to swell and shrink in a cross-grain direction, but will be relatively stable along the grain direction.

Veneers for use in plywood are primarily harvested from the trunk by means of a rotary cutter. The trunk is clamped by two centered pins that spin it against a long stationary blade. As the trunk is spun, a continuous veneer is unrolled, much like paper off a roll. The veneering unravels the tree fibers at 90 degrees to the unrolling action. By alternating the grain direction of consecutive veneers in plywood, the tendency of a veneer to move will be kept in check by the next layer and vice versa. This technique is called cross-graining and is usually applied at a ninety-degree angle between veneers. The alternation of the grain direction of consecutive veneers—as in the warp and weft of weaving—produces a wood sheet of great shear strength and dimensional stability.

Timber is cut to size, debarked, steamed, and readied for veneering

Veneering by means of a rotary cutter

Stack of veneers

## HISTORY

Events representative of a society's values write themselves into history. We choose what to include and what not to, and frequently rewrite history as our values change. In light of this, Nikolaus Pevsner's 1939 essay "The History of Plywood up to 1914" marks a milestone as a first writing of plywood into history—a promotion of plywood from simple matter to a matter of cultural significance.[2]

The following "History of Plywood" should be viewed in this light: as a reflection of the values, aspirations, and ideas of the research that follows. It is presented in a loose chronological sequence, which has very little value other than as a catalogue of ideas.

Modern plywood, as we know it today, is a rather new creation. The first patent for plywood was issued December 26, 1865, to John K. Mayo. The use of the term "plywood" is itself even more recent. Previously it was known by a variety of names, including Veneered Limed Board or Veneered Stock among others. Veneer, however, had a pejorative connotation—"...to disguise with artificial attractiveness" was the 1931 Chambers's *Twentieth Century Dictionary* definition.[3] Seeing this as a hurdle toward widespread acceptance of the material,

First advertisement for new plywood quality standards

Veneers are graded and stacked

Pressing the veneers into panels

Pressed plywood panels

industry adopted "plywood" (until then an obscure scientific term) to describe its product. In 1919 the Plywood Manufacturers Association succeeded the Veneer Association, marking a milestone in the popular growth of the material.

Plywood technology, however, is by no means recent. Veneers and lamination techniques have been used for thousands of years, primarily as a way to optimize the use of rare woods. In fact, they can be traced at least as far back as ancient Egypt, where we find our first evidence of the use of plywood. In his 1948 edition of *Ancient Egyptian Materials & Industries*, A. Lucas refers to a six-ply wooden coffin of the Third Dynasty (2980 to 2900 BC) from Saqqara:

> The sides, ends and bottom of the coffin...consisted of six-ply wood...None of the pieces of wood was either broad enough for the height of the sides, nor long enough for the length of the coffin, and in order to obtain the necessary height, width and length, separate pieces of wood were joined together by means of flat wooden dowels, which were held in place with small wooden pegs. The different layers making the thickness were also pegged together, the various layers being arranged with the grain of the wood alternately in different directions...[4]

This description shows that the Egyptians recognized both the principles of plywood—veneering and cross-graining—and its potential. This technology could help them make not only stable boards, but also continuous wood surfaces that exceeded the dimensional limitations of the tree.

The knowledge of cross-graining for *strength* is also documented in antiquity. Vitruvius clearly refers to the stabilizing properties of cross-graining in his *Ten Books of Architecture*. In Book VII when writing about flooring, he instructs: "... after finishing the plank flooring, lay a second plank flooring over it at right angles, and nail it down so as to give double protection to the framework."[5] This cross-graining keeps in check the "...swelling with dampness...shrinking from dryness...sagging and settling" he refers to earlier. Whether it involves Egyptian dowels, Vitruvius's nails, or modern plywood's resins or glue spread between sheets, cross-graining, to be effective, requires an element of continuity between the grains.

Veneering, cross-graining, and forming were, however, craft skills—skills that until the beginning of the Industrial Revolution were tightly guarded by individual artisans. The Industrial Revolution and the invention of woodworking and wood-processing machinery created new possibilities, including the development of the technology of presses and veneering machinery, and later of glues and resins.

Sir Samuel Bentham, Brigadier-General and Inspector-General of the Naval Works of England in the eighteenth century, is recognized as having advanced, far more than anyone else, the state of woodworking machinery. In order to employ unskilled prison labor in wood construction, Bentham developed a series of machines that automated tasks previously performed only by skilled artisans. His work laid the foundation for the adoption of plywood as an industrial product. Wood left the domain of the hand and entered the machine age. However, wood did not, and still has not, crossed over completely. These apparently dichotomous characteristics are beautifully embodied in plywood.

It was not until 1890, with the invention of the rotary cutter,[6] that large veneers could be harvested to manufacture plywood sheets of exceptional size and strength—the first examples of our modern plywood. Advances in other fields were also critical. Once veneers are harvested, pressure is required to laminate the sheets and assure a good bond. Throughout history, pressure has been applied in

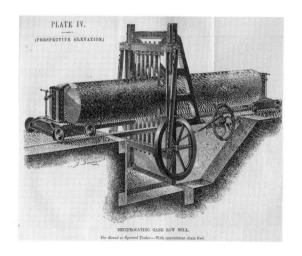 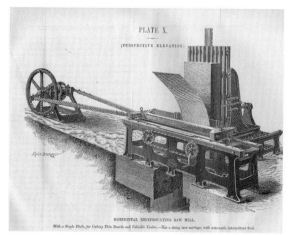

Image at right: Reciprocating Gang Saw Mill. Image at left: Horizontal Reciprocating Saw Mill

a variety of manners, through the use of weights, clamps, or screws, and other hand devices. The invention of the hot-plate press was critical in the transformation of plywood from a locally applied artisan technique to an industrially manufactured product. It was also critical in achieving very strong and lasting bonds. The hot-plate press method is clearly described in a patent issued to Christian Luther in 1896. He later developed this technology at his factory in Reval, Estonia. His seats for bentwood chairs were among the first examples of industrially manufactured molded plywood. Plywood as an industrial *sheet* product made its debut at the turn of this century in the tea and rubber chest industries, providing simple, strong, and inexpensive boxes that could be efficiently shipped flat and assembled on site for the return shipment of goods.

It was, however, the aircraft industry and the great demands made on it by the World Wars that radically transformed and advanced the nature and technology of plywood. Not only did these pressures produce more advanced forms of plywood (for example, in synthetic, waterproof resins and high-frequency electromagnetic curing technologies), but they also radically transformed it from a sheet good to a

Napco Aircraft Plywood Logo

molded product of great sophistication. Invention of the flexible bag vacuum presses transformed wood-bending technology (developed by Samuel Gragg and Michael Thonet, among others) into molding techniques for complex curves in plywood. The DeHavilland "Mosquito" plane, for example, was entirely fabricated in plywood. Malleable, light and strong, it was the ideal material for free-formed aircraft bodies. Furthermore, the uniformity in engineered characteristics assured plywood full membership in the automated fabrication process. Critical here was the adoption of grading systems by the industry. Plywood leapt from being inconsistent and character-driven to being uniform and homogeneous, both prerequisites for mass production of engineered products. The abundance of wood

Mosquito Aircraft

and its low cost were also factors. Manufacturing a wooden plane also meant that the war industries could employ less skilled workers. Unlike metal fabrication, basic woodwork required little skill, and for the more demanding tasks the industry could tap a large pre-existing reservoir of carpenters. In the factory and on the field, a wooden aircraft could be built or repaired with basic saws and hammers, requiring little skill and time. Plywood aircraft technology was a great combination of high and low technology. Whether used by cutting-edge technology or the layman, plywood was a very undiscriminating material. Its abundance coupled with its embodiment of democratic values has contributed to wood's (and plywood's) popularity and legacy in American history and culture. One would be hard pressed to find anyone who has not worked, in one way or another, with wood. This direct physical experience shared by the population at large, coupled with its tactility, bestows on wood a collective familiarity: a familiarity that, one might argue, fuels the "warmth" of wood.

Capitalizing on this rich material legacy, Lawrence Ottinger, President of the United States Plywood Corporation in the 1940s, speculated on the future development of "plastic-plywood."[7] In his article "Plywood's Future has just Begun,"[8] Ottinger's prognostic was far-reaching. His inventory of plywood technology is extraordinary—plywood bath tubs, feather-weight automobile bodies, aircraft shells, indestructible furniture, and other real and speculative applications. Plywood was not just an inanimate material to him, but somehow was able to capture his imagination and sail on the flagship of modernity, embodying all that was desirable: lightness, strength, malleability. In his article, Ottinger suggested that the then current applications and technology had only begun to scratch the surface of "plastic-plywood's" unexplored possibilities. In making his case, the

Plywood radar dome and plywood tubing

article presents present and speculative plywood applications through a plethora of technological examples: from advances in molding to advances in the material composition. The ability to endow wood with previously unknown attributes goes hand in hand with the development of manufacturing and fabrication technology. New technologies, like DuPont's "transmuted wood," promised to re-engineer properties of wood, rendering it stone hard, heat resistant, and absolutely stable.

Suddenly plywood held promise as a polyvalent material. It could hold any form and any physical characteristic. This promise, unfortunately, did not have its opportunity; plywood was soon cast aside in favor of plastic. Cheaper, stronger, more malleable, now plastic's quantitative characteristics seemed to promise the most for the future. Outgrowing its parent, it appeared as the new, true, polyvalent material. It was, however, predominantly a quantitative polyvalence, suggesting that progress could be furthered by a reduction of human experience to the quantifiable, without considering the *quality* of that experience.

BENTWOOD PRECEDENTS

## SAMUEL GRAGG

SIDE CHAIR, AMERICAN, CA. 1815–1820

American-born Samuel Gragg developed sophisticated bentwood technology, receiving a U.S. Patent in 1808. It would not be until some fifty years later that Michael Thonet, experimenting with laminating strips to attain curved wood elements for his chairs, reached a sophistication in bentwood on par with Gragg's.

An outstanding example of early bentwood furniture, Gragg's side chair reinvents the relationship between legs, seats, and back. No longer seen as distinct elements, they become one and the same form, sharing both visual and structural connectivity. The figuration of the three parts in the sinuous S-curve is expressive of a resolution of simplicity. The idea of continuity through simplicity is furthered by the back legs. Bent and spliced in the back they suggest a figuration that is both part of and separate from the larger S-curve. This dual reading suggests a moment of delamination, where one becomes many, a vision explored some 116 years later in Aalto's Paimio chair drawing.

Samuel Gragg, Side Chair, bent ash and hickory, courtesy of Charles Hitchcock Tyler Residuary Fund No. 1, Museum of Fine Arts, Boston

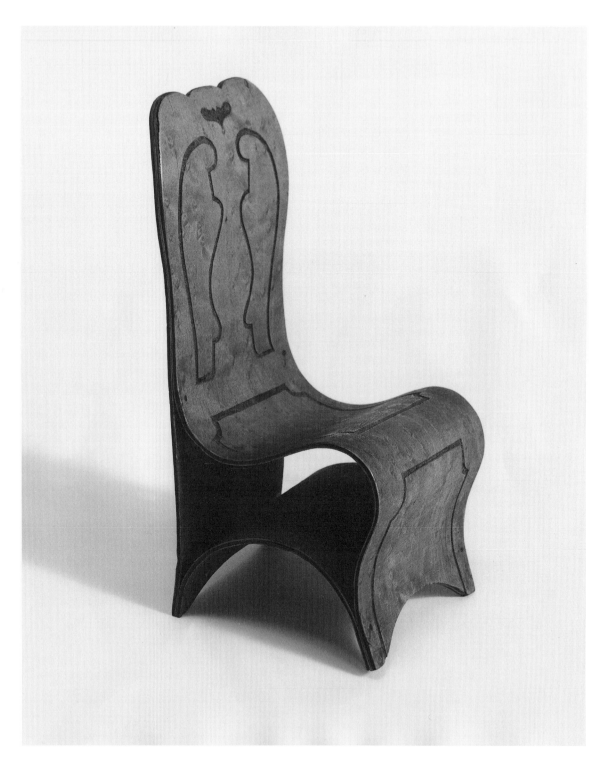

ISAAC COLE

PATENT MODEL FOR ONE-PIECE PLYWOOD CHAIR, AMERICAN, 1873

Cole's patent model for a one-piece plywood chair is one of the very first examples of a molded plywood furniture piece. The design takes the idea of laminated bentwood and applies it to industrial plywood. The reference to the industrial product and the way in which Cole chooses to resolve the issue of rigidity are ingenious. Folding discrete sheets, he relaminates the points of contact (feet and back) and in doing so creates a continuity in which the void under the seat is understood, not as a leftover but as a positive figure of space *within* the sheet. By binding the three components of back, seat, and legs within the material manufacturing logic itself (through relamination) he inextricably binds them both structurally and operationally—the chair is truly a one-piece chair.

As with the Thonet chair, Cole uses the curvature of the seat and overlaps to create rigidity. He also doubles the material at the greatest points of contact of the back and feet. Sectionally the model also suggests some of the ideas, such as a strategic building up of section, developed by Aalto in his Paimio chair.

Isaac Cole, Patent Model for One-Piece Plywood Chair, molded plywood in three sections, courtesy of The Museum of Modern Art, New York, Purchase Fund, photograph © 1998 The Museum of Modern Art, New York

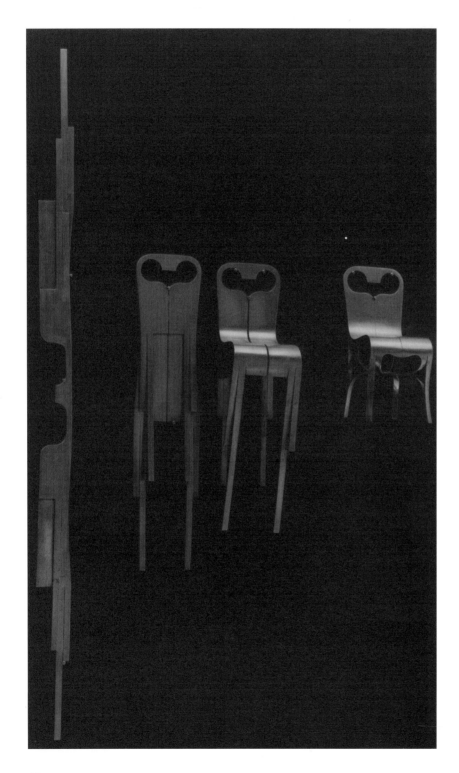

## MICHAEL THONET

### EXPERIMENTAL CHAIR, AUSTRIAN, CA. 1875

Thonet's Experimental Chair is certainly one of the most astonishing examples of nineteenth-century technological innovation in chair manufacturing. Conceived as a continuous laminated bentwood piece, the chair is built up of sheets measuring almost eighteen feet. Each piece makes up a half (split along the middle) of a chair. Template cut and bent, the pieces fold on themselves like intricate origami figures. Front and back extensions fold under the seat and overlap with the legs to provide great rigidity and strength. Arguably an early precursor to the complexly folded continuous wood laminations found in designs such as Frank Gehry's furniture for the Knoll collection, the chair brings to resolution the idea of a simple economical means of production and the reinterpretation of carved woodwork traditions and decorative motifs through the use and development of industrial manufacturing processes.

The folding model sequence represents the process of bending and cutting, while the chair itself expresses the idea of folding and overlaps used not only to stabilize the legs but also to double the material thickness in the back portion for added strength.

Michael Thonet, Gebrüder Thonet Experimental Chair, courtesy of Gebrüder Thonet GmbH

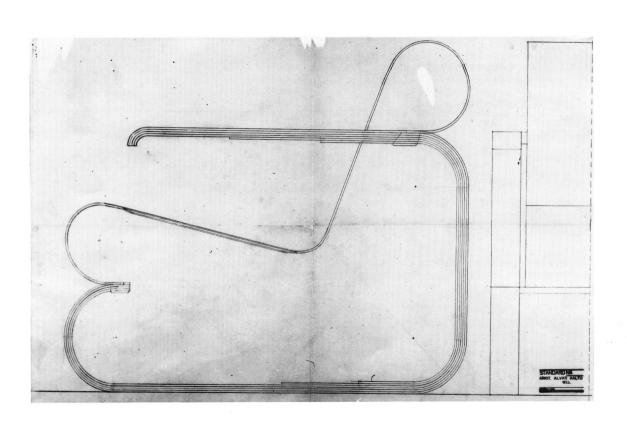

## ALVAR AALTO

PAIMIO CHAIR, EARLIER VERSION, FINNISH, 1932

Perhaps more interesting than the chair itself (which differs from the drawing), are the propositions presented in this drawing. The drawing suggests an idea of laminations that join, envelop, and part in a figure of changing section and undulating curves. It expresses the polyvalent qualities of laminated wood both in form and in fabrication. The laminations continuously respond to the changing, local, programmatic needs. Staggering the joints helps strengthen connections and emphasizes the continuity over distinct parts. The thinness of wood in the back piece exploits its elasticity for comfort, the built-up seat provides extra rigidity where needed, and the thickness of the built-up frame changes in response to comfort and load transfers from chair to floor. Curves are added for continuity of elements and to impart sectional rigidity to the seat. The parting and coming together of the laminations renders a figuration where seat, armrest, and legs become inseparable. This is made possible by considering each lamination as a "programmed" participator in the chair figure, informed in shape and allegiance by its functional requirements.

Alvar Aalto, Design for an alternative version of Paimio Chair, courtesy of the Alvar Aalto Foundation

**GERALD SUMMERS**

ARMCHAIR, ENGLISH, CA. 1934

Designed for tropical climates, this hardware-free chair is an outstanding exercise in simplicity through a carefully calibrated series of cuts and folds. With the complete industrial sheet of plywood visible, the chair tests the limits of its integrity. The minimization of labor and parts and limiting the fabrication process drive the design. The ingenuity of the chair is possible by fully understanding the industrial quality and manufacturing process of the sheet and exploiting its logic. The tropical application of the chair further challenges the design, as attachments, fabrics, and any external fixtures are weak points that would enable humidity to penetrate the artifact and rapidly decay the chair and delaminate the wood.

Although minimal in its manufacturing process, the design did not fare as well economically as one might expect, resulting in a chair that cost more than the leading alternatives. Despite this, the chair possesses a vitality and tension that are as current today as they were in the 1930s.

Gerald Summers, Armchair, courtesy of the Mitchell Wolfson Jr. Collection, The Wolfsonian–Florida International University, Miami Beach, Florida

## CHARLES AND RAY EAMES

MOLDED-PLYWOOD LEG SPLINT, AMERICAN, 1941–42

More than any other plywood product, the Eames's splint attests to the technological sophistication reached in molded plywood technology during World War II. It challenges the sheet-like nature of the single veneer. It establishes a way to address the problem of making compound curves with a sheet product by the careful removal of material to free a second direction of curvature. There is a complexity of joinery, overlap, and addition of material where required by structure and form. Furthermore, the complexity of form attained makes for great sectional rigidity, clearly expressed in the achieved material thinness. The Eames Splint is also a remarkable innovation that expresses the optimism toward the use of plywood, especially in aircraft design, in the 1940s.

> Today plywood is a factor in the manufacture of every product that requires a combination of strength, lightness, and durability.[9]

Charles and Ray Eames, Molded-plywood Leg Splints, courtesy of Eames Office © 1999 www.eamesoffice.com

PLYWOOD WHEELCHAIR PROTOTYPE

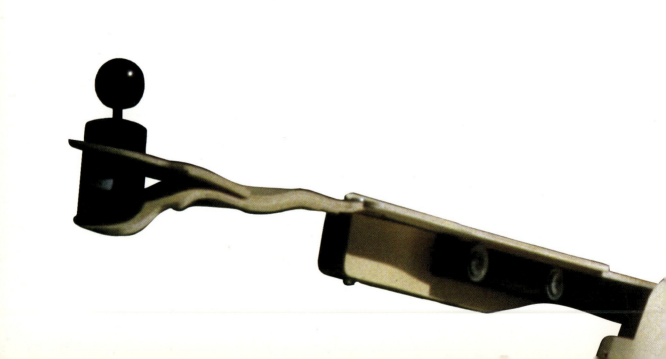

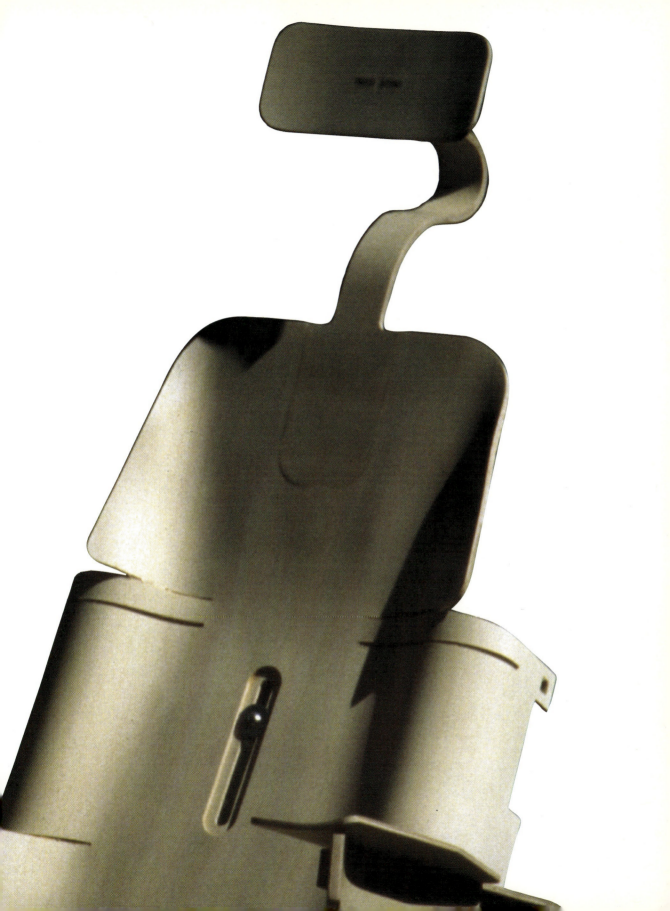

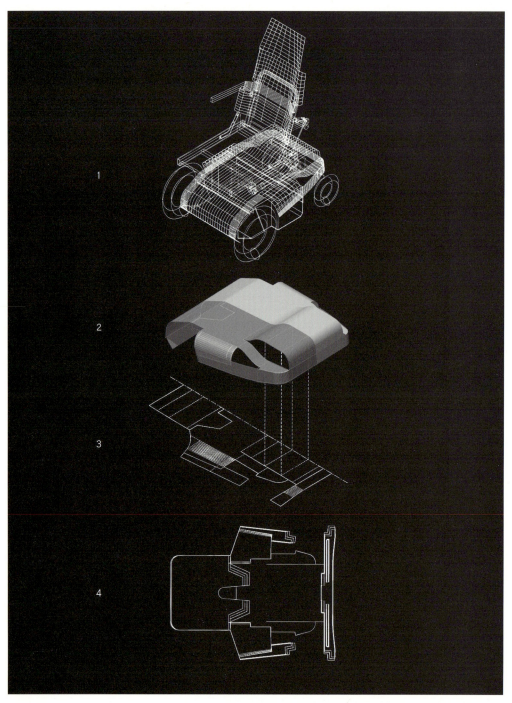

(1) Wire-frame model of chair, (2) surface model of wheelchair base, (3) drawing of half of base unfolded, (4) drawing of full series of unfolded and overlapping sheets

## APPLIED RESEARCH

In any design, materials must respond to functional needs. The wheelchair's function required that plywood achieve the flexibility and strength of plastic. Plywood's bending radius (about two inches with thin birch) and bending characteristics (along only one axis at any given point) presented limitations. The research built upon existing bentwood and plywood fabrication technology. To produce complex curvatures, a way to translate three-dimensional surfaces into flat cutting patterns had to be devised. By cutting veneers with an "orange peel" pattern (a strategy used by cartographers in mapping the earth), the project hypothesized that the laminates could be pressed into approximations of compound curved surfaces. This process would, however, preclude a high level of precision in mapping and cutting the patterns. Each segment would have to fold perfectly on itself. Not only that, but because of the thickness of the curved material, each subsequent laminate layer would have a slightly different profile.

The great complexity and precision required (both in computation and fabrication)—from the analysis and milling of the complex patterns for individual veneers to the fabrication of precise molds needed for their lamination—was made possible through CAD/CAM technology. For one finished prototype more than 70 patterns needed to be cut, accounting for about 300 layers of veneer. This process guaranteed a complex and continuous plywood mold that could be serially produced in an automated environment.

Furthermore, the CAD/CAM fabrication system deployed by the research constituted an iterative process by which multiple modifications could be rapidly implemented and tested. It also suggested the possibility of customization within a mass-produced item. For example, this design strategy allowed a range of parameters to be implemented and thus, for example, a seat could be custom-fabricated to fit the contours of a specific user. The design itself remains the same, with the numerical values of the parameters of that design changing. Other fabrication techniques (such as laser etching) and the use of chemically impregnated fibers further expanded these computer-elaborated characteristics of wood.

Conceptually, however, it was important to provide a level of performance in wood beyond the aesthetic: one in which wood and program could be inextricably bound to each other. This new performative dimension was furthered by our surgically intervening to embed the electronic interfaces (such as the motor and directional controls) of the wheelchair *within* its wood surfaces.

Performance study of translucency of plywood

## PROCESS

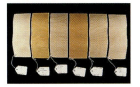

(Top) Minimum curvature test, (middle) surface deformations, and (bottom) finish samples

The applied research began with an examination of the performance characteristics of plywood. Minimum bending radius and thinness, for example, were studied in a series of tests and evidence of the material's performance was gathered. Other tests studied the finish quality of the material, or possibilities of laminating foreign materials into it. Other explorations were undertaken to uncover evidence that could answer a number of lingering questions: Were any compound surface deformations possible and to what extent? If not, which strategies could address the issue of compound curvatures?

If we were to produce this new chair through a computerized process, limits of the material had to be quantifiable. Other explorations were geared toward evaluating the quality of both the process and the end product. The evidence gathered revealed the material's performance parameters and helped us establish computer-generated models that were not only dimensionally accurate, but also materially accurate.

We looked closely at plywood's other attributes—the wood's lightness, opacity, translucency, softness or hardness to the touch—in essence all that this wood product could do independently of any form that it held. These attributes were collected and compiled as a *performance matrix*.

Study drawing for unfolding a model

Another part of the initial approach involved analyzing the performance demands first of the wheelchair then of each of its discreet components (armrest, control panel, seat, etc.). Each of these parts was then determined to have qualities that the wood could address. Our *performance matrix* informed us, for example, that the control panel would need numbers 1, 2, 5, 6, 8 of the material attributes. This abstraction freed us from thinking of the chair only in terms of existing forms and produced a performance catalogue that could inform our form.

APPLIED RESEARCH   45

**WHEELCHAIR PROGRAM PERFORMANCE MATRIX**

Wheelchair

Seat              Base

Armrest        Light fixtures
                      Wheel covers
Backrest       Casing

**PLYWOOD PROPERTIES**

1        Lamination—insertions within
2        Dimensional stability
3        Suppleness + instability of single veneer
4        Rigidity + strength of a built-up section
5        Ply-ability
6        Tactility
7        Flexibility
8        Translucency of single veneer

| COMPONENT | PROVIDES |
|---|---|
| **Armrest** | |
| 1 6 | controls wheelchair through panels |
| 6 4 7 | comfort |
| 2 4 | supports arm |
| 2 4 1 | supports full weight of body |
| 2 4 | contains person in chair |
| 2 5 6 7 2 | supports other activities—resting of objects, attaching bags, etc. conceals hardware |
| **Backrest** | |
| 4 7 2 | protects back of chair |
| 2 7 4 5 | provides support for padding |
| 7 2 5 | conceals hardware |
| **Light fixtures** | |
| 8 5 1 7 | illuminates |
| 8 1 | signals |
| 2 3 7 | conceals hardware |
| **Wheel covers** | |
| 7 4 | mud-guard |
| 2 4 7 1 | conceals hardware |
| 2 4 7 | protects from wheel |
| **Casing** | |
| 7 2 4 | weather protection for hardware |
| 4 1 2 7 | conceals hardware |
| 1 2 5 7 | access for servicing |
| 2 | ventilation |
| 1 2 4 7 | protects hardware |

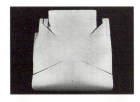

Reiteration of seat component, drawing indicates test corrections. Drawing of final form of base piece below.

The design and fabrication of the chair was by no means, however, a linear process. The computer paired with our material tests could only take us so far. At times we had to infuse our forms with on-site knowledge. The seat is a perfect example. The computer was used to mark up a preliminary strategy of folding. A central arch and side profiles, combined with key locking points, were modeled. Once fabricated, the model was corrected by seated tests and our changes were drawn directly onto the shell. Newly revised data was then transferred back to our computer model. This process continued back and forth until we had a prototype that could address both local and overall design needs. This also guaranteed that our criteria for evaluating the designs were always informed by the demands of the design context. Form was never evaluated solely for form's sake.

## FABRICATION

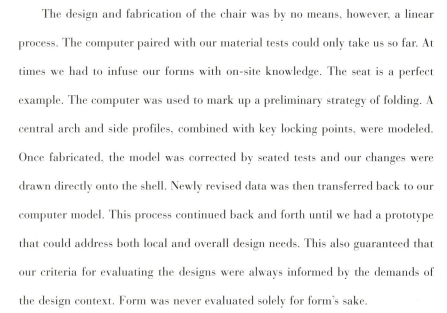

CNC Router

Molds were fabricated out of both one-half-inch and three-quarter-inch Medium Density Fiberboard (MDF), while the molded plywood was built up from flat sixteenth-inch aircraft grade plywood sheets.

Using the same computer model, files for fabricating both the mold and the pieces of the plywood shell were extrapolated. All of the plywood templates were cut on a Computer Numerically Controlled (CNC) router, using a sixteenth-inch carbide tip with all of the MDF scored on a laser cutter. The scored MDF was then cut on the bandsaw, the groove left by the laser catching and easily guiding the blade for an accurate cut. This process was developed to expedite the cutting process as the laser would not have cut through the full stock, and the router was simply too slow for these pieces. The resulting level of resolution of the cut pieces was precise enough for the purpose of the prototypes.

Initially all of the MDF was scored and labeled using the laser. The pieces were then run through the bandsaw and readied for assembly. According to the laser-etched number on each piece, the molds were then assembled without glue by means of the slotted connection. This allowed for any of the inserts to be eventually replaced with a slightly different section. The mold was ready for use.

The wood sheets followed a similar process. Each 2' x 4' sheet was placed on the CNC router bed. The computer file was run, and the carbide tip cut smoothly through the wood. Some pieces were sent through a second process in which they were processed through the laser cutter for etching. The oval *Permobil* company logo, as an inextricable element in the wood, was prepared this way, as were some of the techniques elaborated for allowing the wood to perform beyond its normal limits. Pieces were labeled for easy assembly and correct allocation with each corresponding mold. The sheets were now ready for pressing.

Most of the plywood forming was completed using a vacuum press. A dry run was performed before actually applying resin between the veneers. Once the sequence was clear, the resin was applied. Each interior surface was skim-coated, the sheets were arranged in the correct sequence (including touch-sensitive membranes, etc.), and placed on the mold. Pre-designed alignment guides allowed the sheets to be placed correctly relative to the mold, which also prevented them from sliding once in the vacuum bag. A compressor, attached to the plastic vacuum bag, removes air from within it. As the bag shrinks down it distributes pressure evenly, pressing down the veneers to conform with mold. Pressure was applied to the bag and mantained for about three hours (enough for the resins to cure), after which the pieces were removed, ready for assembly without requiring additional tooling. Finish coats were applied and the pieces were ready for final assembly onto the chair.

(Top) CNC router cutting a laminate layer, (middle) full set of laminates being formed on the vacuum press, and (bottom) molded piece with its formwork

## THE MOLD

(Top) Bandsawing the laser-etched mold profiles, (middle) slotting the mold together, and (bottom) a completed mold

The same computer model that was used to generate the laminar cut-outs, was used for the mold. Sliced like a loaf of bread, the model was cut into a series of cross-axial sections. Each section was extracted from the model and turned, through simple rotation, into a flat cutting pattern. Each section was fitted with an interlocking groove. The sectional profiles were, as with the laminates, cut out with the CNC or laser cutter. When cut, the groove allowed for an interlocking assembly of the parts to make a solid gridded mold. The resolution of the selected grid is dependent on the resolution of curvatures and thickness of the material being pressed. Like miniature corrugations, the infinitesimally small undulations imparted onto the molded shell by the ribbed mold increase the sectional rigidity of the piece as a whole. MDF was chosen as the formwork material for its great homogeneity, ease of cut, and stability.

As products of a direct process from computer to cut patterns, the accuracy of the mold and laminate profiles was a near perfect match. Furthermore, unprecedented accuracy allowed us to embed electronics or to inset hardware elements into the wood. Ultimately, this process guaranteed a very precise and complex (both in form and performance) plywood shell.

## THE LAMINATE

Cutting material out to relieve two directions of curvature

The fabrication of the chair began with the raw product: wood. Early tests showed that the use of single veneers would prove problematic. The unbound veneer was unstable and undulating in nature. If the computer was to cut a direct translation

APPLIED RESEARCH   49

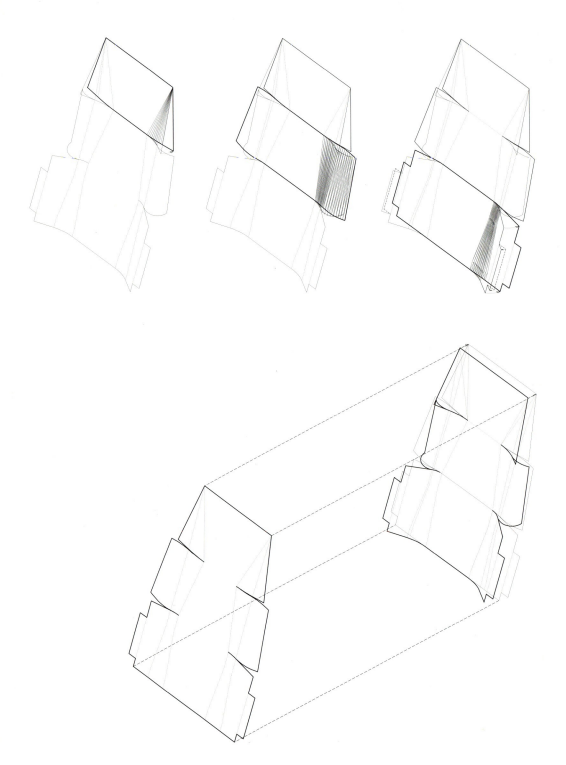

of a series of flat drawing instructions, the material would have to be perfectly flat. Even the slightest surface undulation could translate into a critical distortion in the cut piece.

Aircraft grade plywood was chosen for its near perfect stability and flatness. Its thinness was comparable to that of a raw veneer (one-sixteenth of an inch) and its unblemished and perfectly homogeneous composition would guarantee it great success in the automated and serial manufactured process.

Once models had been developed on the computer, their surfaces were built up to the thickness of material required at each point—in effect transforming a surface into a shell. Not unlike the skin of a piece of fruit, the shell was "peeled" sheet by sheet, into a flat pattern. For this part of the process a peeling system had to be devised that could not only translate the surface parameters with infinitesimal accuracy, but that could also be automated. Eventually the process would be automated algorithmically. A process of faceting (or very close approximations of straight edges) was used to fold the curves into the cutting plane. Each layer would be slightly different as it reflected a slight change in curvature. A system of joinery, where the surface dimensions exceeded the dimensional limitations of the 2' x 4' plywood sheets, also had to be devised. Complex overlap patterns in three dimensions were created to impart the greatest structural and material connectivity. Finally, a series of distinct cutting layers was produced that was essentially a series of offset plan views of each layer. The data was sent to a CNC, or laser cutter. These cutters, like plotters, follow the pattern defined by the computer program. With router bits or a laser, rather than pens, they "draw" through, cutting the material. The result is a series of flat sheets that will eventually be pressed into a mold.

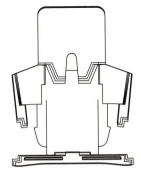

Drawing of overlapped series of unfolded sheets for base of the chair

Left: drawing of the unfolding sequence for the back of the chair

APPLIED RESEARCH 51

COMPONENTS

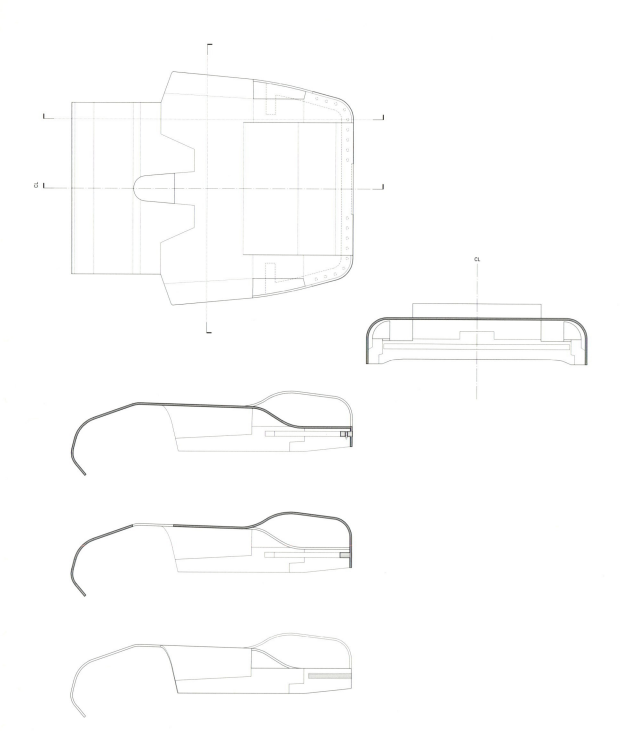

BASE

The plywood shell base for the chair wraps around to shield the chair's computer and driving mechanisms. The shell is a two-part assembly, the front slipping off and unlocking from the back for maintenance access to the chair's mechanisms. The front is notched in at the point where it meets the chair piston, and curves around and under the front of the carriage. The top portion of the back bumps up to hug the contours of the computer, in the process giving the shell greater rigidity. The side apertures are covered by acrylic operable panels that provide an internal view of the chair and space for recharger cables and attachments. The triangular corner insets double as part of the shell's locking mechanism and as external electrical input connections. The input devices include a recharge plug, and data and voice connections for computer servicing. The back is connected to the steel frame by means of a plate. A layered lamination of acrylic and wood sheets, the plate forms a locking mechanism with the two long slits. The plate is also the chair's rear brake light. Embedded lights burn bright red and form a set of shell-flush brake lights. At the rear of the back, between the slit apertures for the interlocking connector and brake light plate, is a laser-etched *Permobil* logo. The traditional set of external attachments such as lights (boxed-out plastic cases) and logo (in the form of a sticker) have now been fully integrated with the materiality and fabrication logic of plywood.

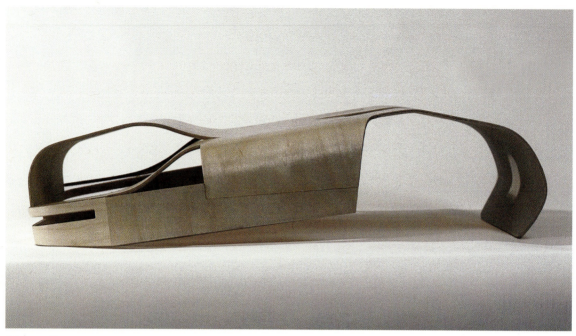
Side view of base

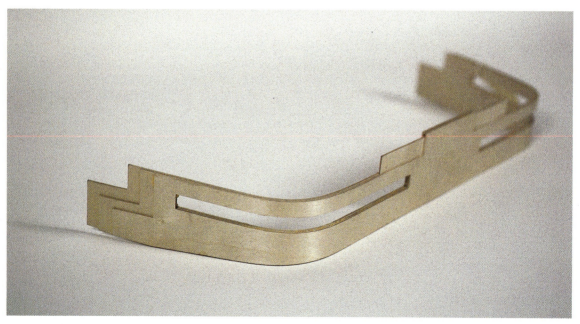
Rear portion of base prior to final lamination, note stepped connection at sides and middle to ensure a strong connection

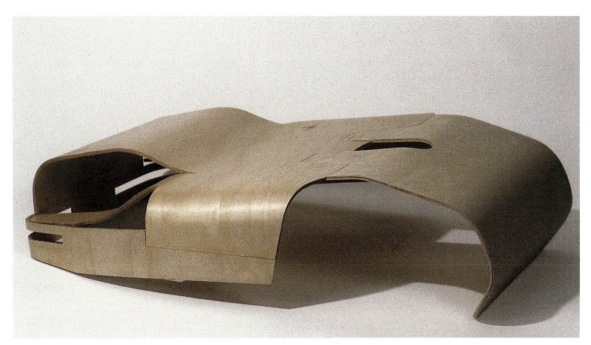
Three-quarter view of base

Rear half of base, note company logo laser-etched between the connector slots

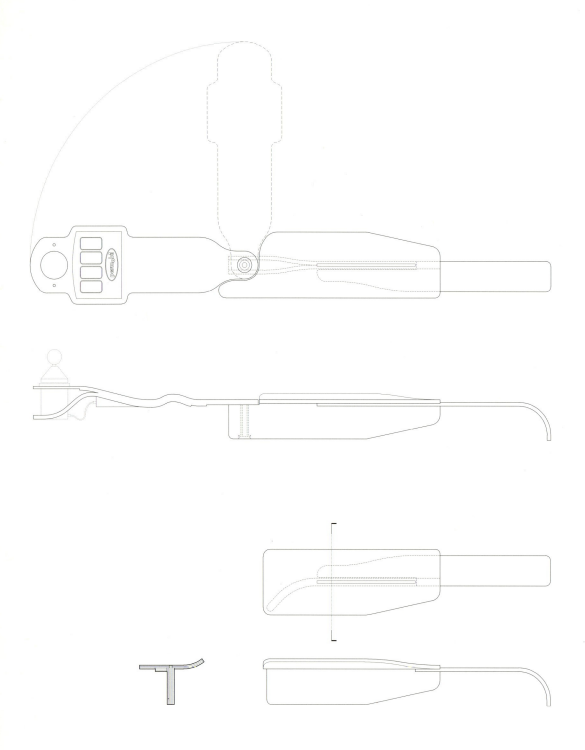

ARMREST AND CONTROL PANEL

The armrests comfortably cup the user's arms in place. The side connector plate tabs into the armrest in an exposed end-grain connection. With humidity the end-grain tends to expand, further strengthening the joint. The connector plate curves slightly outward after it has made sufficient contact with the chair frame. This outward curving provides lateral support to increase the stability of the connection. The armrest for the control panel splays open symmetrically to allow for a laminated tubular metal sleeve and pin for the pivot connection. The control panel is free to pivot outward to a ninety-degree position so that the chair may be brought into maximum proximity to tables without the panel getting in the way. A stop on the left of the panel prevents it from swinging in front of the user. The panel itself undulates to impart sectional rigidity in response to the positioning of the arm. The first undulation supports the wrist, then raises the etched function buttons to a comfortable use-angle and then bends back to brace the joy stick. The bottom portion delaminates to make space for wiring and to support the bottom of the joystick. Internal membranes and wiring transfer the electrical impulses through the control panel, across the pivot, along the armrest, and out the back to the wheelchair computer. The embedding of a laminate of circuitry and sensors allows the user to control the chair through physical contact with (the new touch-sensitive characteristics of) the wood.

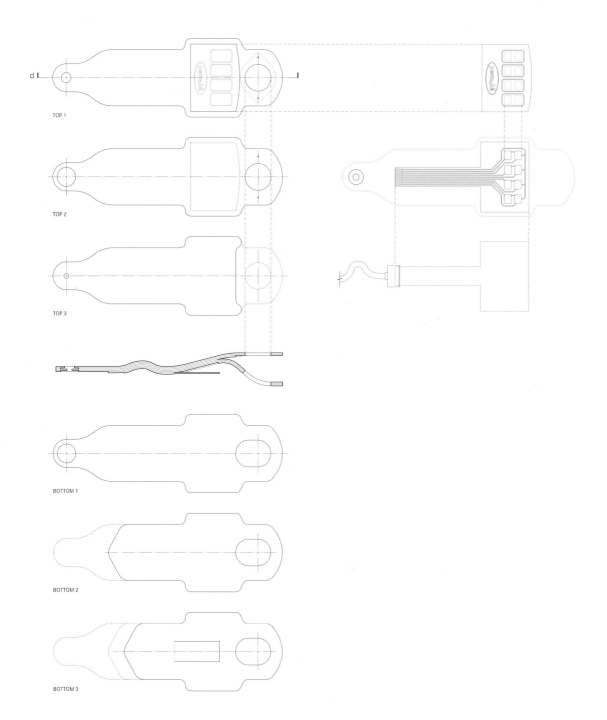

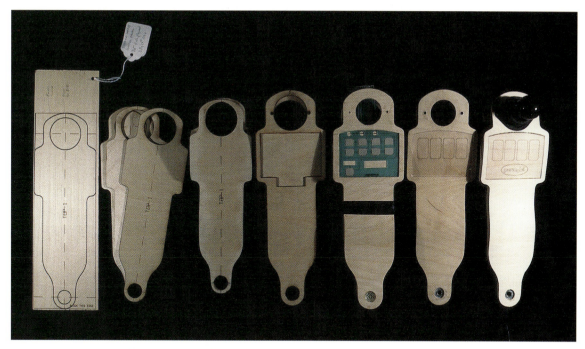
Sequence from flat sheet to final prototype, note embedding of membrane

Final control panel prototype, note the wiring entering the laminate

COMPONENTS

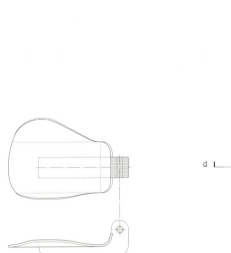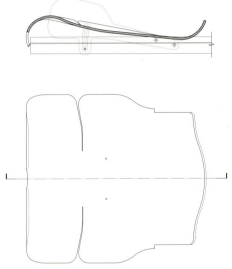

## SEAT AND FOOTREST

The seat follows a three-part sequence. The back portion cups up to provide a comfortable end-support, the center folds up at the sides to provide lateral support, and the front creases in the middle to make room for leg support and curves around the front to support the inner knee comfortably. The front is notched as it folds underneath itself to make swinging room for the movement of the footrest post. The seat is supported on the underside by three ribs that connect it to the frame, securing it at a slight incline toward the backrest for greater comfort and user stability. Side louvers can be raised to provide further side support, comfortably supporting legs that might otherwise flail apart. The louvers can then be pushed down to create a flush seat surface for easy user movement out of the chair. The louvers are pivoted around the back, and are secured by stabilizing the sliding connection at front to hold it in place. Formed as a series of S-profiles the louvers fold in from the frame to hug the sides of the legs. The footrests are attached to the post by means of nylon sleeves laminated within the thick L-profiled connector. By means of the pivoted connection, the footrests may be folded up. The footrests are tabbed into this bracket with their upward cross-cup, holding the foot on the plate. The plate cups in a secondary, and perpendicular, direction for a slight compound curve of great rigidity.

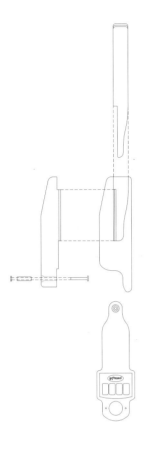
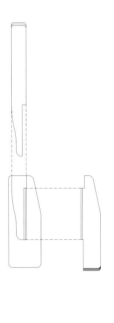
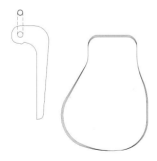

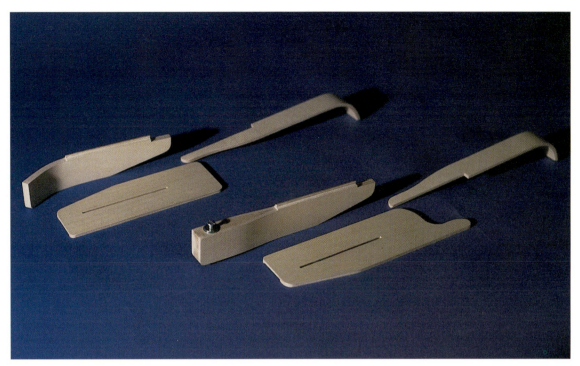

Disassembled armrest components

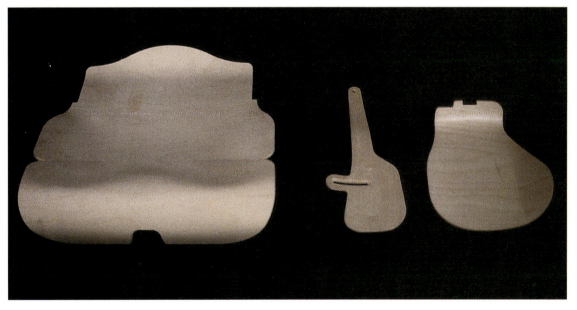

Seat, seat louver, and footrest

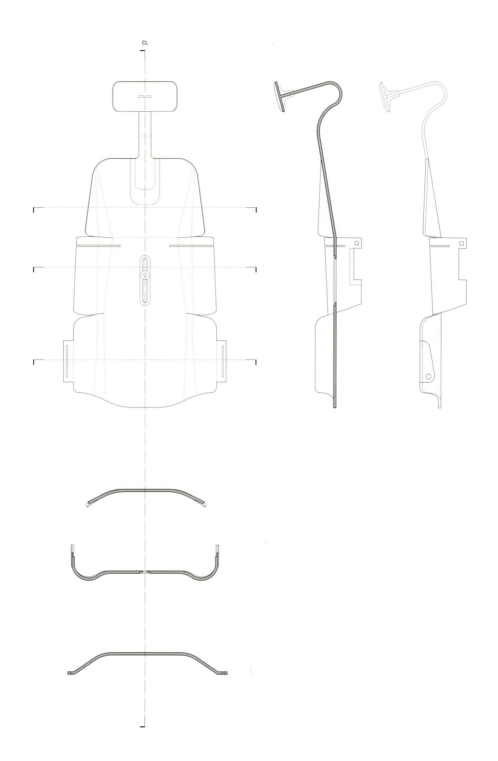

BACKREST

The backrest is also based on a three-part logic. The top portion cups in for great sectional rigidity and shoulder blade support. The center portion supports the length of the back then bends backward to embrace a space behind the chair's frame. The top slit and side holes are connectors for future sets of attachments: computer racks, telecommunication devices, storage units, etc. The connectors allow for easy lock-on and lock-off. The side holes click onto pins, the slits help stabilize and secure the edge connection to the backrest. Exploiting the flexibility of the wood, a simple outward pressure on the side tabs liberates the attachments from the pin connectors. The bottom portion of the backrest cups inward to provide comfortable support to the lower back. A centrally located groove allows for a sliding connector to the chair frame. Two side connectors slip through the bottom side slots for a strong end-grain connection. These connectors bolt to the pneumatically controlled side levers that tilt the chair up and down. The top portion of the backrest is spliced with an undulating element that folds over to connect with an end-grain connection to the headrest. The curved undulation provides a flexible, yet strong, support. The headrest plate is further stabilized by a lapped vertical brace. Ultimately, taking a lead from the electronics of the control panel, one could adapt the backrest with an internally laminated heating circuit. Lamination experiments suggest that embedding new synthetic laminates into the wood could endow the surface with a desirable, and controllable, level of ergonomic comfort.

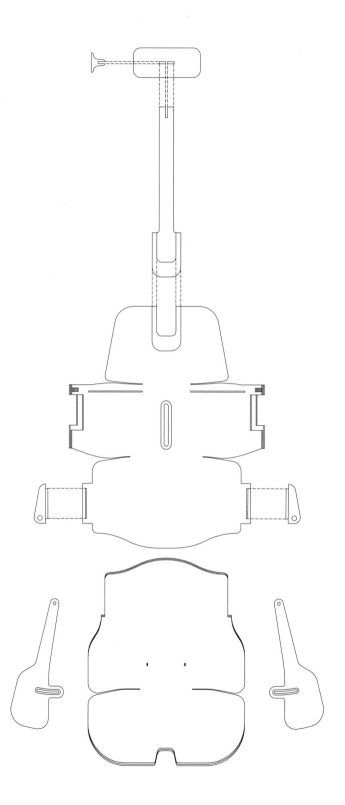

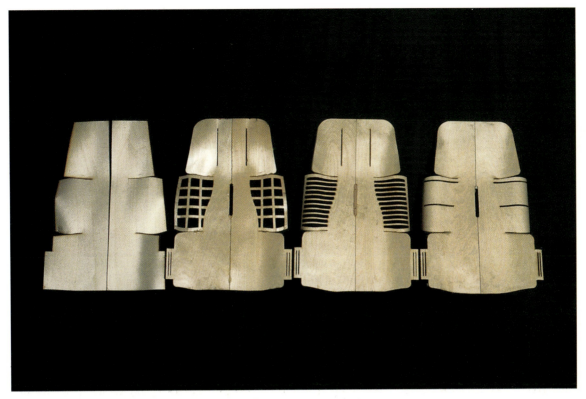
Backrest prototype sequence—from basic parameters to completed piece

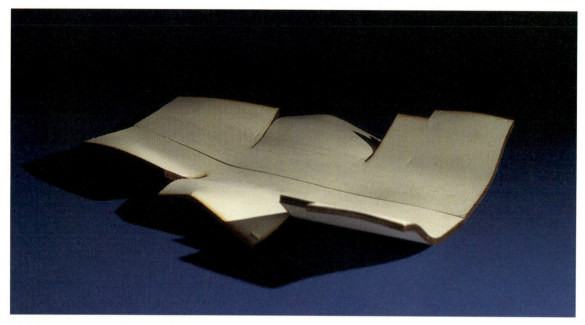
Preliminary parameter-driven backrest model

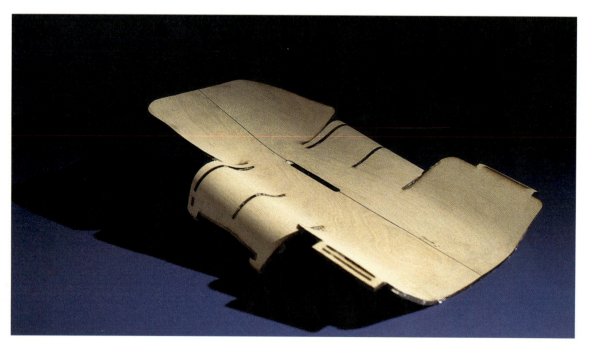
Final backrest prototype, including all connector slots

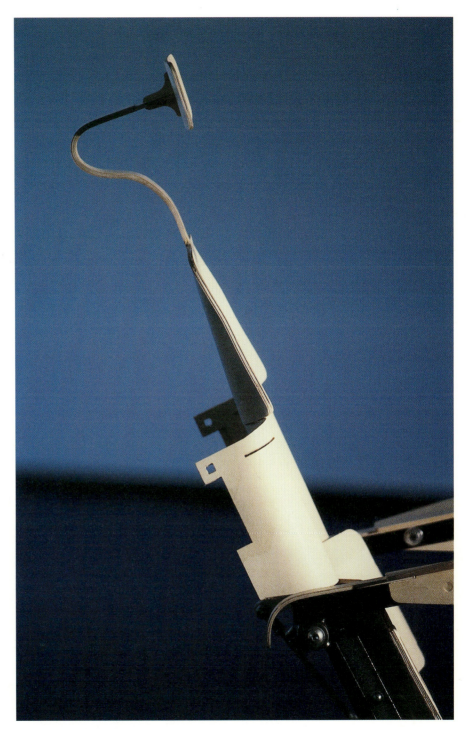

The back and neck rest

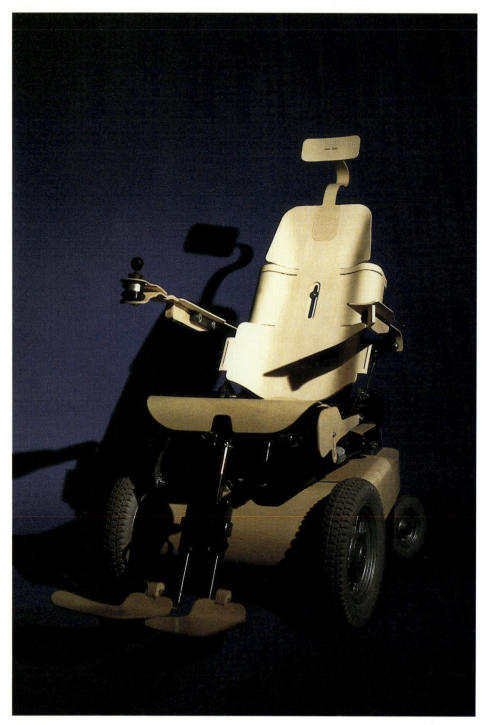

Front view

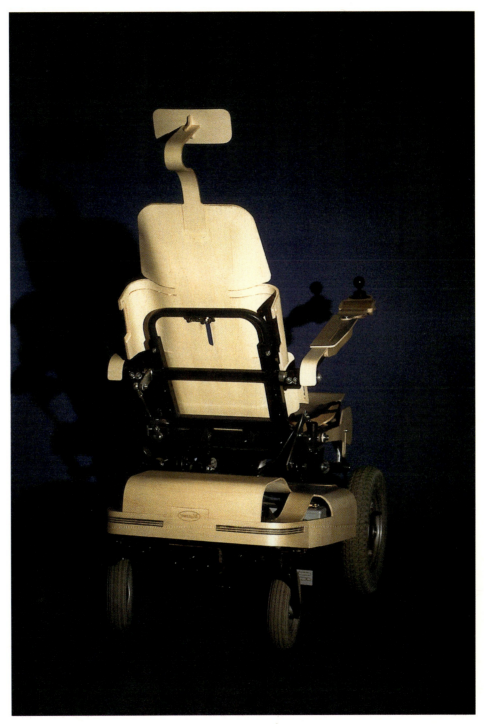

Rear view
Image on following pages, 1/16 inch plywood cut-out sheet set for a complete wheelchair

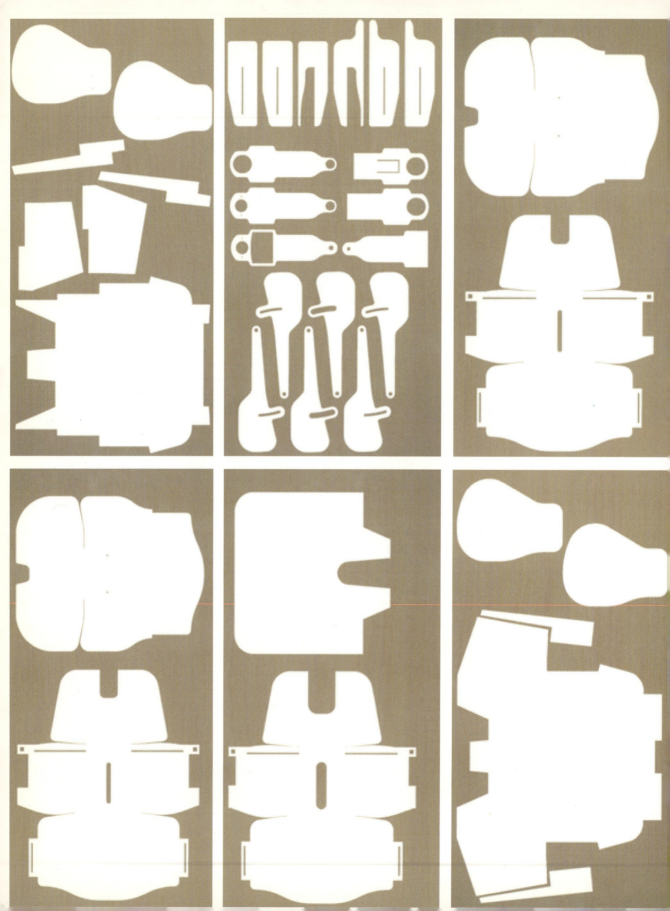

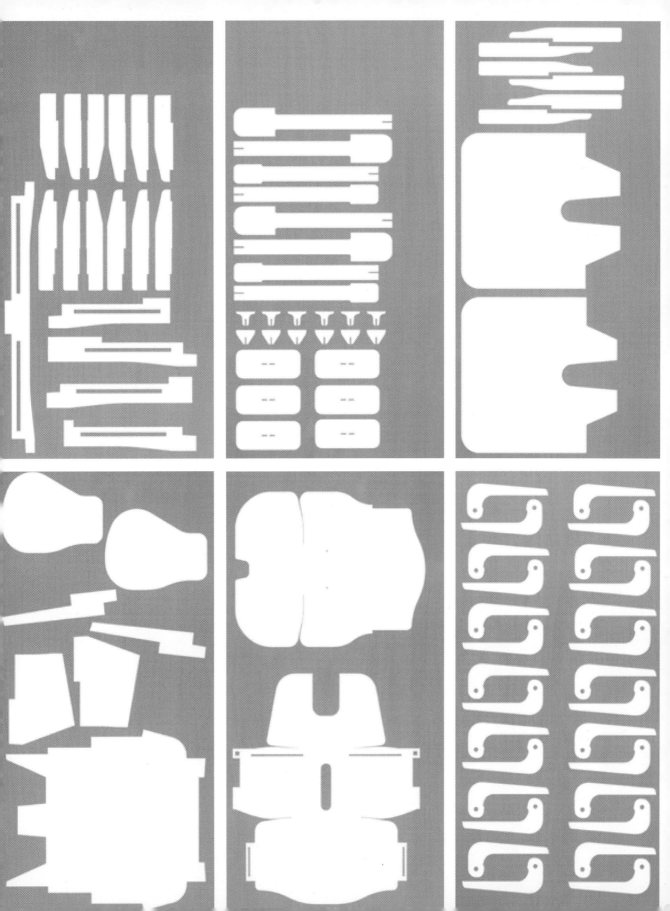

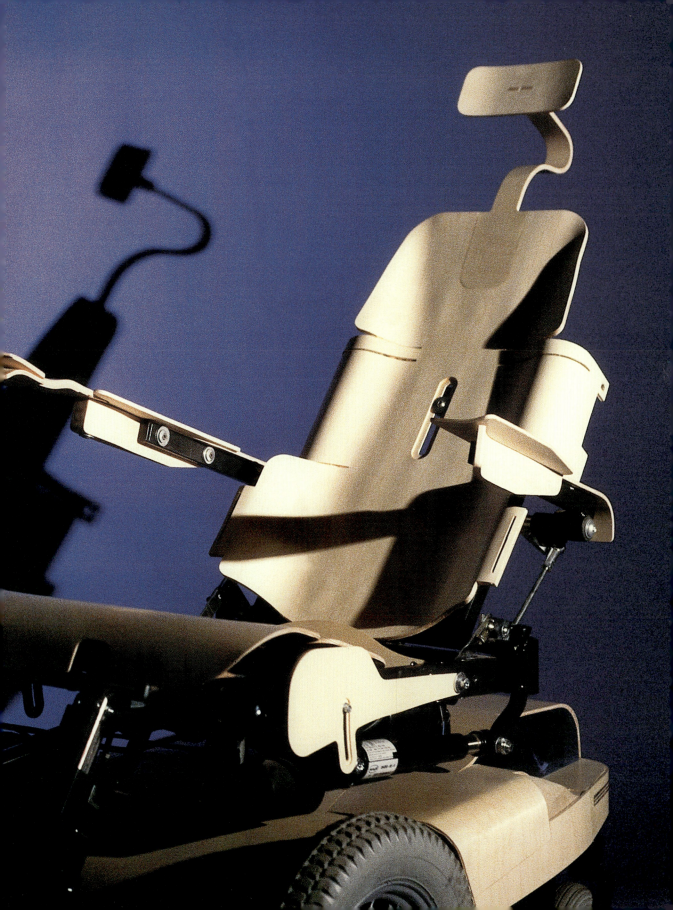

ENDNOTES

[1] James Marston Fitch, *Architecture and the Aesthetics of Plenty* (New York: Columbia University Press, 1961), 272.

[2] *The Architectural Review* 86 (September 1939). This article was an adaptation of "The First Plywood Furniture," which appeared in the August 1938 issue.

[3] Andrew D. Wood, *Plywoods: Their Development, Manufacture, and Application* (Edinburgh and London: W. & A. K. Johnston, 1942), 7.

[4] A. Lucas, *Ancient Egyptian Materials & Industries* (London: Edward Arnold & Co., 1926), 511–512.

[5] Vitruvius, *Ten Books of Architecture*, trans. M. H. Morris (Cambridge: Harvard University Press, 1914).

[6] Wood, *op.cit.*, 5.

[7] Plastic-plywood refers to chemically impregnated and altered plywood that acquires plastic-like characteristics such as great malleability and strength.

[8] Lawrence Ottinger, "Plywood's Future Has Just Begun," *Pencil Points* 25 (May 1944), 79–84.

[9] Louis H. Meyer, *Plywood: What it is. What it does* (New York: McGraw-Hill 1947), iii.

ILLUSTRATION CREDITS

Pages 12, 47 (center), 50–51, 54, 58, 60, 62, 64, 66, and 68 drawn by Mark Careaga

Page 16–17 (bottom), courtesy of Rutland Plywood Corporation

Page 17 (top), courtesy of American Plywood Association

Page 20 (top), John Richards, *A Treatise of the Construction and Operation of Wood-Working Machines* (London: E. & F. N. Spon, 1872)

Page 20 (bottom), Aero Digest's *Aviation Engineering* (New York: Bryan Davis Publishing Company, June 1941), 208

Page 21, courtesy of Mosquito Aircraft Museum, London Colney, England

Page 23, courtesy of American Plywood Corporation

All other images © 1999 Marco Steinberg

*Dean, Faculty of Design*
Peter G. Rowe

*Director of Lectures, Exhibitions,
and Academic Publications*
Brooke Hodge

PUBLICATION CREDITS

*Graphic Design*
Margaret L. Fletcher

*Project Assistance*
Michelle Fuson

*Printing*
Bolger Publications/Creative Printing

PROJECT CREDITS

*Client*
Permobil USA, Inc.

*Concept Initiator and Grant Development*
Natasha Makowski, Lionheart Gallery, Boston

*Principal Design and Research Investigator*
Marco Steinberg

*Research Assistants*
Mark Careaga
Chris Cooper
César Quiñones

Special thanks to Sheila Kennedy, Byron Mouton, Kimo Griggs, Kevin Lair, George Doyle, Mike Newby, Rutland Plywood Corporation, Schauman Plywood of Finland, and the Department of Lectures, Exhibitions, and Academic Publications, Harvard University Graduate School of Design, for their encouragement and support of this project.

**Marco Steinberg is an Assistant Professor of Architecture at Harvard University Graduate School of Design**